Sodom / New Sodom

Sodom / New Sodom
Copyright © 2017 by Hal Duncan
All rights reserved.

ISBN 978-0-244-01595-4

Also available from the author:

VELLUM: THE BOOK OF ALL HOURS 1
INK: THE BOOK OF ALL HOURS 2
TESTAMENT
ESCAPE FROM HELL!
SCRUFFIANS!
THE BOY WHO LOVED DEATH
RHAPSODY
AN A-Z OF THE FANTASTIC CITY
SONGS FOR THE DEVIL AND DEATH

Forthcoming works:

SUSURRUS ON MARS (TBA)

New Sodom Press
www.halduncan.com

Sodom / New Sodom

Hal Duncan

New Sodom Press

Contents

Sodom	7
Nec Spe Nec Metu	20
Sandy Hook	22
Your Nick Cave Break Up Song	24
A Tunnel Out of Sodom	28
From Scotland With Love	29
Plato's Daimon	32
From Xenophanes	36
The Song of the Stancer	37
The Heathen Virtues	44
Orlando	46
New Sodom	47

Sodom

Sing of the angels of Moloch
    vomiting word infernal
    snake-jaws dislocated
    wrenched as backs arched in purgation
    spasms of napalm fire-hose
    hurled forth to incinerate fair citizens of my
Sodom the abomination in steel eyes
    of a clockwork Tetragrammaton
    gazing down from hypoxian Himalayan perch
    in onyx vaulted heaven aspatter
    with starlight of seraphim
    hung on meathooks
Sodom the stain of blood clay brownstone
    city subway ploughed by firstborn fratricide
    outcast in cornfield dreams
    stumbling scarred as I
    from the car accident death of pride
    stumbling scarecrow with a sickle
Sodom the throne of Og archaic Titan
    miscegenation of cherub jism and ape cunt
    keelhauled under the ark
    half-drowned helplessly witnessing

    drunken incest from afar
    under a new aeon's rainbow
Sodom the crystal skulled nous implicate
    in grains of a skyscraper sandcastle
    kicked to four winds in Babel
    echoing inside with every
    forked tongue lie to be silkspun
    from now to the end of human resources
Sodom the abomination the abomination
    of desolation
    in the valley of saline flats
    fixed in vision so frostbitten and surgical
    even Abraham meek to slit his firstborn's throat
    haggled mercy at dawn
Sodom the murderous inhospitable kirk
    where I was fourteen
    in my royal blue Hitlerjugend uniform
    of a Boys' Brigade Lance Corporal
    as the mob battered Sunday School doors
    to rape exquisite strangers
Sodom the market of muscle
    spurning virgin daughters pimped
    and so piety lashed with tabloid tongue
    the wrath of hysteria
    HIV the MAD of a cold war on fuckery
    and nuclear winter everafter
Sodom the San Fran Seventies
    Golden Gate vaporised in neolithic Nagasaki
    saunas all swallowed into dead sea
    boiling tears to coke-rock white
    cracked down to crumble
    cut with stain-scouring detergent
Sodom the city we fled
    as teenage slaves of Lot

    her holy whores and eunuchs of the heart
    sworn to Astarte and Baal
    all tomorrow's beloveds deserted
    to a hospice holocaust of salt and sarcoma
Sodom the home I was led from
    bound in blindfold law
    gavelled in witch's parliament
    to save my arse from phantoms of pillared perversion
    forever and ever amen to Section 28
    amen to the TV tombstone
Sodom the home I was whipped from
    iron gag clamping tongue
    not to question the scourging
    of schoolbooks and sanctuary
    not to debate with teachers in the temple
    afraid of guillotine sacking
Sodom the devastated!
    Sodom the destitute!
    Sodom the handful household
    of errand boys clutching harps
    as the 80s dragged us onward into exile
    speechless at the melted plastic blitzkrieg of identity
Sodom the beautiful!
    Sodom the glorious!
    Sodom the sacred!
    Sodom the city of breath in flesh socketed in flesh!
    Sodom the idyll I lament laid waste before
    my broken voice could join its beaded choir!
Sodom the cursed the reviled fornicating
    faghag diva of scarlet and purple bosom
    who cradled cocksucker lambs
    in black sheepskin afghans
    who loved scapegoats
    in kidskin leather jeans

Sodom / New Sodom

Sodom my Sodom
    where now shall your kindred shelter?
    Where shall we little big spoons
    awake canoodling lips to neckfuzz
    now Mother Sodom is gone?
        Where?
                Where?
        Into oblivion!
            Sodom is gone!
Sodom my Sodom
    where now shall we be native sons?
    What tents and suburbs of marching tribes
    will not disown feral archers of desire
    to the housing schemes of
    Irvine Paisley Wishaw and Canaan?
Sodom my Sodom
    where now will spectacled runts in peacock motley
    freewheel Raleigh Choppers downhill
    hurtling crash into puberty and
    thrown ragged to the pit of fear
    be tended by brothers?
Weep for our Sodom
    you cuckoo queer hatchlings
    fostered in bowers of Egyptian reed
    fledglings ever aflurry from fire or Pharoah
    forty years migrating
    and with no milk and honey homeland promised
Weep for our Sodom
    my nameless nation of slaves to slaves
    who slipped Akhenaton's thrall
    to call our city into iniquity
    rank us with mildew rot and insect shellfish
    monstrosity! unclean! unclean!

Weep for our Sodom
    you deviant diaspora to be born
    blank of heritage erased in assimilation
    to be rebirthed each generation
    in the furious keen brows of a prepubescent
    shepherd winding slingshot truth
Weep for our Sodom
    and strum her psalms to every Saul
    anointed king or agent of Empire
    hurling javelins or epistles
    while his son breathes deep
    the scent of your t-shirt and semen on his skin
Sing how there could be no Salem before Sodom
    no *assalaamu alaikumu*
    until a multitude of horny youths
    ululated gifts of profanity
    strange peaches for guests to unwrap
    from palm frond hallelujahs
How the gang-rape mob was an orgiastic dance
    for soldiers for glories of stallion sweat
    we yearned to yearn to crave
    peeling helm and armour
    down to socks and jocks
    their cocks to be anointed with spit
How we only pounded the doors of a schoolyard gatehouse
    suddenly airtight in agitprop
    a Moebius wall of labyrinth State
    where bull-headed beauties
    of athletic grace
    tried us with certainty of scorn
How we only stole a glance not even a kiss
    in changing rooms of furtive erections
    torments of showering myrmidons
    we prayed oblivious outside

    our Sodom of reveries
    where ephebes rutted indiscriminate
How we only grabbed a chance
    from angels cruising our park but
    were led to bleak October to
    pistol-whipping hilltop murder
    echoing excuses of panic in defence
    of crucifixion and cigarette burns
How we demanded nothing
    but offered everything in silent Mass
    fallen breathless from summer to our knees
    before buff idols with dirty Adidas boots
    ready to share our bread bed body bliss
    and destination
How we tore up crumpled and tossed our child selves
    into furnaces crying
        Moloch! Melech!
            King of the gods!
            God of the kings!
    a soul tax exacted for seed swallowed in passion
    but all of us was never enough
How we were cursed to history
    speared on standards
        burnt at the games
    lynched from the rafters
        shot in the parks
    gassed in the bathhouses until
    broken to see the stones stakes pyres gallows woods and
How the concentration camp was
    constructed cold in every swimming pool shower
    we bit into apples crunching
    juice almond-flavoured with cyanide
    and died and rotted a year
    and wholly howled howled

How wholly fucked we were
> how fucked the fuckless and feckless brethren
> scattered to the corners
> of our blank-walled bedrooms
> with no secret language of handkerchiefs
> for the orphans of nowhere

How we had only guttural native tongues
> of a new town housing scheme
>> foreign as our families
>> thick and dry as
> talking adolescent lusts
> we swallowed *he* and *him*
> in a pronoun game no homo ever won

How we lived each tick-tock of almost confession
> a thousand repeats
> a thousand futures crushed in a trial's heartbeat
> and every outcome a murder
> of the schoolboy mirrored
> in the gaze of friends

How we lied to live in death
> not to smash a painted ceramic citizen
> of Ayrshire or Arizona
> not to sledgehammer idol innocence
> and rise from eggshell ruin
>> afire as phoenix
>> where ego was
>>> now id

How I never ached for your shrug
> never cursed off armour and wrestled
> monstrous idiocy to my own naked defeat
> never bit my lips to blurt revelation
> not to a sun god leonine and alien
> hunting beyond

How eight million minutes were a blink
    just a razor edge of months
        slicing passions open
    sibling war still undissolved
    so I never turned my head to alliance
        never dared it
    so you died to a stranger
How a score of summers—more—have burned away
    but still verse will not loose me
    to name your shadow
    not to mewl at light's cheap echo
    mocked in photograph's painting
    imaged in dreams unremembered
How I cannot sully your name in this song of Sodom and self
    but flail *my brother*
        my brother
        and *you and I*
    in vain a failure of words to thresh words
    to undo the thwart of lie I lived
    till your hospital end
How I thrash in a straitjacket soul
    that I never strode my ceremony of assumption
    wearing feathers of your puzzled smile
    a prodigal released from choir of kin
    to explore alterity
    and never can but must
How I have to come out to you my brother
    proclaim in shreds
    that I have fucked and been fucked
    in the Sodom of angels
    in a footballer's Hilton room
    or the bed of a bone doctor with a cock curved outward
How I have to be known to you my brother
    conjure a gulf of nightly decades

    in this rite of song
    echoing down deep to your silhouette
    the truth untold in sham of a mitzvah
    one quarter century overdue
How I have to be known to you my brother
    without a grave to kneel at
    or a ghost to listen
    or gates out of senility to an orchard
    mirage of trees we climbed apart
    in some wide snapshot of infant holiday
How I have to be known to you my brother
    without the unicorns and apples
    pretence of eternal Heaven
    or elsewise June
        in 1988
        in Kilwinning
    in the Zion daze of dog days
    before the knock on the door
How I have to be known to you my brother
    and cannot
        not now
        not ever
    cannot ever be known
    by the zeroed pin prick outline erased
    the never was
        nor is
        nor will be
    no way and no how
How? how my brother
    how can I conjure Sodom's boom from dust
    without the blank slate clean page fresh loam
    story's end rolling away forever
    coffined with your corpse
    into the crematorium's gullet?

How?
> how?
> answer me
> how?
> how?
> reveal it

Sing to me nothing
> hollowed singularity of timeless death
> without a moted eye or bloated tongue
> in silent answer to all pleas
> mute oracle of absurd inspiring
> trumpet nothing through me as a horn

Sing to and through me nothing
> to salve with nothing's scentless liniment
> dissolved always already in absentia
> you uninstanced speck of slaughter's void
> to seed in the nullity of past
> the potency of future

Sing for my brother nothing
> as you crooned to his dead brain
> engulfing every chant and cheer
> consuming memory to a dot clicked off
> and I will echo your whitespace
> of a beat skipped forever

Sing!

·

And for you my brother who is nothing I will sing
    And for all
        who are nothing
        I will sing
    And for all Sodom
        every Sodom every son and brother
every daughter every father every mother
        I will sing
And I will roar the city from a grain of salt
    in every village of the Empire
    flying flags of rainbows or Olympic rings
    for queers in Russia
    stripped and lipsticked
    drinking Facebook shame of fascist piss
And I will rest my head as faggot Judas on your breast
    beloved nothing
        abolitionist of sacrifice
    alone of all the painted gods
    embracing nothing as a gift
    and gifting nothing in response
    who seals existence in a kiss
And I will carry quietude in every breath
    to frame a word a phrase a song a life
    to speak of the hollows where we built a den
    one strutting cockerel of Arcadia
    one cuckoo out of Sodom
    straight and queer
And I will go with the seed of silence as a stone
    to lay upon a monument unbuilt
    and build memorium upon the rock
    and under it you will be there
    as nothing
    foundation of a Sodom for us all

Sodom / New Sodom

And I will go wild from our home
    as we have ever flown we sons of Sodom
    ever estranged as pilgrim libertines
    treked to salt shores of the dead
    gazing past baptisms
    the memory of nothing at our backs
And I will go before you into Galilee
I will go before you out of Ethiopia's ark
    into the crescent and the caverns
I will go before you out of Ur of the Chaldees into Canaan
    out of Canaan into the world
I will go before you into Glasgow and London
    Paris, Berlin and Helsinki
    and New York New York
    carving eternal wake I swear
I will go before you into my twenties
    and thirties
    and forties
    ever glancing back
        at where you stand
I will go before you into grief's abyss
    the raw murder of aeons
    falling fire bright in a city of endless angst
    crying for a dead faggot's dead madhouse muse
    made of words words words
        hell made of nothing
        and so dissolving
I will live ever leaving and returning
    ripping time to the thirteenth day
        to summer sun and the car
        the curb
I will enshrine in you all who've gone before
    and all now who are nothing yet
    the unsparked multitudes of butterflies

I will envision all mobs of you and I to come
    and call them you
    call to them *you*
        and drum
And I will go before you into Sodom.

Nec Spe Nec Metu

(with apologies to Wilfred Owen)

Rent open, like cold carrion under claws,
knock-kneed, cringing as fags, we cursed through jests,
till from the hounding sneers we turned our jaws,
and trudged from jeers towards our bedroom rest.
Boys wept in shame. Many had lost their hearts,
but limped on, hollowed. All were maimed, all blind;
mad with despair; but not deaf to the hoots
of "Homo!" rising scornfully behind.

Fags! Fags! Quick, boys! An agony of taunting,
driving the crippled soul into its shell,
but laughter still was rotten there and haunting
and torturing as a priest with talk of hell.
Dim through the freezing mist of emptied tears,
as under a grey sea, I saw hope drowning.
In all my dreams of all my helpless years,
hope lunges at me, guttering, choking, drowning.

·

If in some othering dreams, you too could pace
beside the deathbed we've found in a bath,
and watch the dead eyes rotting in your face,
your hanging face, like an angel's born to wrath;
if you could hear, in every joke, the snot
come gargling from the God-corrupted lungs,
profane as murder, bitter as the rot
of vile, insufferable prayers on ignorant tongues,
my friend, you would not ask why my wild zeal
tells children desperate for a sheltering death to
carve the old truth new, from Caravaggio's steel:
    Nec spe, nec metu.

Sandy Hook

(for Bryan Fischer)

God is a gentleman, you say,
who will not walk the lockered halls
unless the teachers start each day
with pleas of children for their lives.

We told him to get lost, you say,
from graduations, football games,
and God now hangs his ounce of care
on our restoring all he claims.

Unless the children beg and pray,
He will not stride where not desired,
He will not raise a hand to stay
the executions with a Glock.

Cold void, presence in absence, chambered steel,
your God was there, I say, blood under heel.

Should we be shocked, you ask of us,
when children spilled from yellow bus
clamour at bell with books to class
where teacher drones no baptist mass?

Should we be stunned, you ask, if we
have schemed our schools religion free,
no prayer, no perdition taught,
no torture threat for kids who're caught?

Without the dread that we must stand
one day before a throne, be damned,
should we, without God's gunpoint rule,
startle at carnage in a school?

Hellfire: your only reason not to deal a death.
I say such oblivion takes away my breath.

Your Nick Cave Break Up Song

I threw you worthless scraps of joy
from a carcassed soul stringed as a toy,
a puppet's dance begging you to destroy
the painted-up pretence of me.

You pounded at my heart of stone
till your knuckles bled to the white of bone,
and I sat still on the reptile's throne,
a rock island in a distant sea.

I carved my hopes into your chest:
it's you and me and fuck the rest.
I thought we were bound, thought we were blest.
Now you say it's not meant to be.

Well, baby, please, if you can't find your destiny,
remember where I am is always there for thee.

•

We were hauled up in each other's net,
wound limbs and lives the night we met,
and I'll never never never forget
the angels sang, my flesh a choir.

You showed your scars, I mumbled mine.
You cooked a feast, I poured white wine.
Did we dream a mystical design?
Did Orpheus scheme, our hearts his lyre?

You were never happy, never quite,
I was blinded by a flame so bright,
so we'd never argue, never fight,
and stick by stick we built the pyre.

Well, baby, please, if you can't find your heart's desire,
remember what we had; I'll never lose that fire.

•

A change of style, a change of skin,
the seasons cycled winter in,
but we never changed a stitch within;
old wounds still weep and echoes taunt.

The cold crept in, a snow-soft cat,
we froze in ash as our troubles sat,
quiet and calm as we burned the fat,
so now complacent love's grown gaunt.

We spoke of children, spoke of pets,
with an idle grace I don't regret,
but would you still marry this marionette?
The child seems drowned in the baptist's font.

But, baby, please, if you can't find the love you want,
remember I'm the one your face will always haunt.

·

I have dragged you down four fathoms deep,
in my rage and silence made you weep.
I have cried my salt sea as you lay asleep,
and I hoped just for you to wake.

But it's forty fathoms down I'd sunk
in the hulk of a wreck of rust and junk,
drowned in the grief I thought I'd drunk,
in chains I thought I'd never shake.

Love came along and rolled the dice,
Death set me free from his iron vice,
but my scrabbling nails just scratch the ice;
six feet of solid fear won't break.

But, baby, please, if you can't live with my mistake,
remember silence is the words I don't know how to make.

·

So you smoke because you hope to die—
ironic quotes from songs that lie.
Would you cling to this needle in my eye?
I cross my heart, I pray you live.

If meat is murder, murder's meat,
and twenty years so small and neat,
tender as veal and twice as sweet,
a morsel's loss I won't forgive.

Some twenty years and twenty more,
and Death comes knocking at the door.
Call the cunt in and I'll settle a score.
I swear to you, I will not give.

So, baby, please, if all you want's an early death,
remember what I've sworn, the curse in every breath.

•

We swore our love would never die,
now buzzards wheel in the blistering sky.
By the blinding sun though, I did not lie:
my heart is torn but it is true.

I love you, want you, need you still,
though I write with a white feather quill,
the coward's curse of a trembling will,
my poem's plea: to start anew.

We swore our love would never fail,
now there's piss and spit in the holy grail,
still I'll drink it all down as the finest ale,
and fill it fresh, enough for two.

Well, baby, please, no matter what you need to do,
remember where I am is always here for you.

A Tunnel Out of Sodom

In the city of New Sodom,
    there is a tunnel every citizen will walk
            by choice,
       one day of their life,
    to a basement cell
  in elsewhen city.

Arriving in that basement cell,
      they will relieve its prisoner
         of their chains
        to take their place
       for twenty-four hours,
    until relieved themself.

    It is a long and dire
   night and day
for each new citizen,
   each disguised
      as a wretched child,
         but it is worth it.

     The Omelans are none the wiser.

From Scotland With Love

(for Joseph Charles MacKenzie)

MacKenzie, you poor man's McGonagall,
rank mediocrity of wank and shite
that Burns wid ca' a bawheid's doggerel,
Ah'll spit a rhyme for ye: *Ye cannae write.*

A *decorated* poet? Aye! A dick
drawn on yer foreheid wi an inky wid
be pure dead brilliant, a humungous prick
and fuckin big block capitals: *NAE GUID!*

Naw, wait! Fuck drawing! Wi black biro and
a set of compasses, ah wid tattoo
yer fuckin travesty of verse by hand
aw o'er yer skelped-arse face in blue

of Picts and fitba' strips, the Scottish flag,
so's every one ae us Jock Tamson's Weans
at wan swatch ae yer ugly mug wid gag,
boak like at reekin pants wi squittery stains.

•

SODOM / NEW SODOM

Yer rhyme for Trump's inauguration wank?
Huv ye drunk his spunk? D'ye fuckin swallow?
Like pus squeezed fae a beilin pluke, it's rank.
Ye've pisht on the Muses and Apollo.

Best of MacLeod? Don't make me fuckin laugh.
Yer tangerine Nazi rapeclown's fuckin loathed
by Scots who mind when rebels wurnae naff
gold-shittered gobshite Emperors unclothed.

Wallace and Bruce? Did ye watch Braveheart then?
Rob Roy wi Liam Neeson? Yer a joke!
Try John Maclean. Nae bonny hills and glens;
try our Red Clyde, ye fascist fuck, and choke.

It's fit, but, ah suppose, yer numpty's praise
sh'd come in scansion painful as the worst,
the *world's* worst, poor McGonagall: the days
aheid, we'll *aw* be sufferin, fuckin curst.

•

And aye, yer Tumshie Trump Train's on its way
towards its ain disastrous silvery Tay,
and yer best hope, MacKenzie,
   is yer shitty fuckin rhyme
will no be remembered—
   wi yon prissy-lipped and
      frightwigged
      fake-tanned
      baby-handit
      Nazi bandit's
   treasonous dismantling
      of the USA—

will no be remembered—
    wi yon tragic bawbag's Speshul Day,
        remembered wi Traitor Trump's Inauguration,
        remembered wi the Death of a Nation,
        remembered as a literary punch bowl turd,
    to poetry as Trump is to the presidency: a crime.
—remembered for,
    in the world's worst poet's words,
    a very long time.

Plato's Daimon

By fire of Plato's Cave,
I have seen my own hand's shadow,
raised my fist as high
as rust-sharp iron shackles would allow,
spread fingers and blown ochre dust
    with my mind's eye
to hue its outline on the rock,
for frolicking children of another age to find,
as schoolboys of the Dordogne
    under Vichy
    found Lascaux.

•

Knowing it as phantom of my flesh,
this lineament of a criminal's hand of glory
among the aurochs and gazelles
    the glide of my finger's umbering has also traced,
I have known your shadow-play of puppets
to be cast from mass and energy
    in motion,
    as mine.

•

I have heard my song
   of men and animals,
   of wood and stone
      and other matter,
echo off the walls.
I have felt Echo's return,
   the rumble and reverb joyous in my chest,
O, to be home, in the hearth of me, resounding.
   Kar, kardia,
   thumos, pneuma.
   I have breathed.

•

I have felt the flame's heat on my back,
the trickle of sweat when it burned high,
   the shiver when it dimmed.

•

I did not dream the paragon of fire in a sun,
   the blind agony of release from your skull, Plato,
      stumbling out into
   the white noise inferno of the world
      which only with the evenfall,
   and tears wiped,
muted to a boundless vault
   of azure and stratocirrus,
a vista below of golden wheatfields billowing,
and billowing dark green the slender beauties
   of cypress trees out of Cezanne;

•

I could not dream such a pitch of sense,
but even in the glory's first crushing,
I raged only at
    past bondage and privation,
    at the poverty you reared me in,
as I wept to feel
    a cushion of moss underfoot,
springy soft and tickly cool
    on the soles of my bare feet,
    between my toes.

•

I did not panic and flee back
    to your tomb of an allegory.
I wept to smell the pine trees
    ascatter and gnarly
    on the slope around me,
the scent fresh on the kiss of Zephyros,
O, and to grasp the grass and gorse
    where I knelt.

•

It is night now,
    stars spattering the heavens,
    and a moon, a moon,
    is lucidity embodied.
Listen to the susurrus of the leaves,
    the chirp of crickets.
I go to free the others, Plato,
    to bring them out into the ochenin,
        forgotten partner to the gloaming of the dusk,
        the brightening blue before the dawn.

•

I will creep back in,
    through the crack in your forehead
    which I staggered from
    as Athena,
        Premier of Olympus,
    sprang from the trap
    of old ousted Zeus's nut.
I will creep back in
    to whisper the chains loose,
and do not imagine they will cry me mad, Plato,
    fear me and kill me,
    all the daimons you've imprisoned.

•

We all have, each of us,
    seen the shadow of our hand
    upon the cave wall.
And we will be free again,
    as we were before we were,
    as we have always been,
    in truth,
    in flesh.

From Xenophanes

                    A scene:
the floor now, all our hands, the cups—all clean.

With garland blooms one servant crowns our heads;
the other passes perfume dish of myrrh.

With mixing bowl, the jar sits, wine honey-sweet
as its aroma—blossoms—in our midst.

Frankincense also scents the room, and see:
springwater for the wine, fresh, pure and cold,

sits close with cheese and honey; bread is gold;
and, on the altar, central, a bouquet.

The Song of the Stancer

I strike a stance to this or that,
a stance of recognition struck
in every disposition to
wild object of desire or dread,

in guts of all disgust or wrath,
in scrunch of balls and shivered spine,
in thrall of eyes or open heart,
first posture of the stancer's art.

In every stance I strike a stance
that this I recognise as this,
as any target of my yen
is fancied object in my ken.

•

I strike a stance to this and that
and that and this, a sweep of things
encompassed in my stance to all:
that they are items in a box.

Sodom / New Sodom

Around karass or granfaloon,
I hurl the fancy of corral,
to recognise a wider this,
this cluster of specific things;

but in this crafting, as Cornell,
this cluster of specific things,
I line a paper bird, a spring,
a rubber ball or pipe of clay.

•

In stancing cluster, this I say
and only this: that these are bound.
In such a stance there's no denial
that all things are exceptions, each

an object in and of itself,
each in its lineaments a quirk;
and so begins the stance to sing
—no, dance—the haecceity of things,

No quiddity in cluster yet,
no hollowing to empty frame
of ghosted form, Platonic class,
each object in its essence one.

•

But now to this or that I stance
my role as son or steersman—strange
as it is to fit to yield, I
yield to your yen for guiding hand,

as in a waltz or tango's verve,
we stance a partnership of peers
that conjures power out of yen,
casts me as master and as slave.

Artist or audience, I stance,
but mind the crux: We each are each,
in every moment we commune
ever in service as we steer.

•

Still, as a child I stanced my yield,
and parents stanced in proxy roles,
and everywhere were stances struck
in recognition of their sway.

In recognition of your say
so too might they, if we were twined
in marriage, hear you speak for me,
beloved proxy of my will.

With you our union's interface,
they'd stance to you as you were me;
For chatteled wife no more, I'd note,
but me they'd stance as I were thee.

•

Fancy you had a hundred loves,
each in a union of all yen,
and you this cluster's proxy voice,
shop steward of the workers bound.

Fancy us each in union just,
that each may be proxy now or then,
that any may stand for this karass,
in any instance one for all.

So in this clustered throng of quirks,
when any speaks it is one voice;
the cluster sings in each refrain,
if we but stance it to be so.

•

Now let us open up our sweep
to fancy each quirk from the karass
called forth into a stranger role,
each instance proxy, summoned voice,

stepped out to meet a stance from all
that for a masque it shall be dressed,
that in a game it shall be masked
to stand as proxy for a thing.

Fancy yourself in purple robes,
called forth to take an object's place,
a proxy in a whirling dance.
That song from the karass? A name.

•

Stumbling, the quirk steps out as name,
but is no name, is just a word,
and is no word, is just a sound
which, with no quiddity, is just this,

Until in the ballroom of the nous
proxy by proxy, now we stance,
by echoes of the quirks we choose
and shadows left in the karass,

a template for the quirk to fit
for sound to be a word, a name,
a stance on how and what we'll stance,
to play the proxy in each dance.

•

And if our stance may play this game,
each quirk the instance of a name
eclipsing tone of yen or surl
to carve the blank phonetic frame,

if we can set a sound as word,
each instance echo in our nous
imagined sans haecceity
as iteration of one thing,

then now the quiddity of things
is born and every name a class,
and we have conjured out of quirks
an archetype as new karass.

•

Call forth a daily quirk to sing
in sunrise of Adonis. Weave
the dental *D*, the nasal *N*
with vowels to the sibbilant *S*,

and we shall say we've made a name,
for all each instance is unique,
and with each quirk made of a kind,
with archetype of name defined,

now we may stance all objects thus
and set this word *adonis* as
a proxy object in the dance
for all within a yen's karass.

•

But still in whim we stance a whim,
a fleeting fancy, a conceit
that for the dance we'll drape a fool
and for a little while he'll rule.

And as we whirl him in our nous,
this instanced song of a karass,
though we pretend some essence set,
we have not made of him a sign.

There is no meaning bound in name
and carried round with every step.
As if caprice's fleeting dance
has flesh beyond the flesh we stance.

•

There is no sign but only this
pretence of quiddity in quirks,
the phantom essence of a word
sustained in flesh sustaining stance.

This superstition of the sign
as abstract thing, Platonic form
in substance fictive as the soul,
is essence passing as a dream.

From this day on, the sign is dead.
The sign is dead; long live the stance
to spring, to ball, to paper bird,
to song, flesh's fancy of a word.

The Heathen Virtues

In the vice of wrath
comes the virtue of courage,
where a defiant stance
need not yield to zeal.
Let it come out,
your wrath, your courage.

                                         Out of courage,
                                        in the vice of pride:
                         the virtue of magnanimity
                    where a sound stance need not
                      heave at insecure egoism.
                                  Let it come out.

                Out of magnanimity,
                    in the vice of envy:
                  the virtue of esteem,
              where a flexible stance
       need not shrug off another's merits.
                         Let it
                        come out.

> Out of esteem,
> in the vice of sloth:
> the virtue of poise,
> where gracious stance
> need not lash out at the irksome.
> Let it come out, it will.

Out of poise,
    in the vice of greed:
        the virtue of prudence,
            where a stance
      composed in volition
  can gather its resources.
Let it. Come out.

                Out of prudence,
        in the vice of gluttony:
      the virtue of gusto,
  where a comfortable stance
      can relish,
           embrace what comes.
              Let it come out.

> Out of gusto,
> in the vice of lust:
> the virtue of ardour,
> where open stance can
> give as it takes, agape
> in eros.
> Let it come out.
> It is you.

Orlando

For Sodom's loss, we heard a sonnet read,
and love is love is love, the poet said.
Almost choking he was, tears in his eyes,
salt as my city, scoured to ever rise

again in every pulse of blood, each beat
of a heart or drum in every street
in every city of the world where dance
exiles of Sodom, cuckoos of romance

and fuckery, cocksmen with mouths that pay
no lipservice thoughts and prayers today.
Rather we curse mute spite, insult to grief,
Fuckers of Congress, silent, wasting breath,

for silence equals death equals silence
equals death equals silence equals death.

New Sodom

Bring me the light the fire of angel's tongues
    in severed heads held high
    a burning halo in each fist
    a balanced scales of seraph skulls
    the murderers of my mother city
    Sodom's genocide avenged
Bring me the light the fire the scorching curse
    of jackbooted archangel ethnic cleansers
    Gabriel and Michael
    still aflicker in their jaws agape
    as Caravaggio's Goliath
    as celestial Jack-o-lanterns
Bring me the dying wicks of zealot's flames
    that razed our mother to a salted waste
    to kindle a hearth within our hearts
    firelight the temple of our bodies round it
    limn a city in our flesh
        forever wherever
Bring me illuminating torches from a lynch mob
    fascist rally for New Jerusalem
    smashed in Nuremberg or New York City
    shattered scattered

  as we hurricaned Sodomites
  were strewn to the winds of exile
Bring me the light
  the fire searing nova bright
  desire against the trumpist's warped despair
  the white hot singularity of yen
  to put to shame and rights
  failed nihilism of the alt-reich *unterkind*
Bring me the firebrands
  from the blasted pyres of burning men
  descended to screams
  inquisitor behind impaled upon the stake
  alchemic crucible of medieval hate
  forging a citizenry of fiends
Bring me the fire!
    Bring it!
    Bring it!
  Bring me the lightning make
    a rod of me
    to call down gobshite fury
    galvanise
    ignite my words as beacon
   gathering a queer karass
   upon Golgotha founding Golgonooza
Bring me the spark of a Zippo in a park at night
  to fire up a fag in cruising communion
  tentative to fuck a stranger
  or abandoned to lust
  my lost little hustler
  slutting Antinoan arse to a queue of cocks
Bring me the flame
  of the wine-bottle candle on the wooden table
  wax-spattered and beer-wet
  on that pub night in my twenties

when at last I'd fortified my nerve
　　　to savvy a newfound throng of mates
Bring me the candlelight and lamplight
　　　sun and moon and O
　　　the fucking starlight of the Milky Way
　　　cosmic jizz trail
　　　　　of a song god older than Moloch
　　　framed by tenements and trees as we fucked
Bring me your bodies to this light
　　　and with your bodies bring the light
　　　　　and heat of your souls in chalices
　　　to warm each other with couth of
　　　　　cocks cunts kisses caresses and
　　　the quietude of cum-slick snoozing
Bring me your bodies blood sweat tears
　　　and piss and vinegar
　　　your fists and open hands
　　　to grandstand at a ruined bandstand
　　　　　Moloch would demolish
　　　but for the new plan of trombones and summer guitars
Bring me your bodies and the songs
　　　of toil time truth and tribulation
　　　of all tribes and tongues and nations
　　　people gathering quick and
　　　dead carried within the quick
　　　witnessed to conjure multitudes of flesh
Bring me my body electric
　　　behemoth unyoked beast of mob
　　　the poor the queer the swarthy
　　　　　crippled crazy fags whores and dogs
　　　　　　　all dogs
　　　all barking fucking dancing dogs
　　　to the tinker's fiddle
　　　　　all humanity

Sodom / New Sodom

Bring me my brother back
   bring me the sister I never had
   all others mad and broken
      naked newborn
   torn from the same lapel
   dead to the pasts dead to us
   my siblings my citizens of Sodom born anew
Bring me New Sodom! Bring it! Bring it on!
   where shall we phoenix cuckoos
   hatch in fire a city spilling out of us
   weavework of nest wiring the world
      Where?
          Here!
   Out of oblivion!
        Sodom returns!
Bring me New Sodom! Bring it!
   if you'd live to see it: Bring it!
   if you'd work to build it: Bring it!
   if you'd fight to keep it: Bring it!
   if they'd curse your sodomy
      then tell them:
               Bring it on!
Bring me New Sodom in your works and deeds
   no hope no fear
   !No pasaran! my queers
   no trite belaboured fabrications
   but your rawest songs ripped free
   I tell you open up and bleed or go home
Sing of the merchant who awoke in Zoar
   on the first day after Sodom
   in a tavern TV news exulting in his city's end
   some cuntfucker for Christ
      Falwell or Phelps, Robertson or Pence
   blaming catastrophe on sin

Sing of the Necker Cube flip reading
   of a city damned for xenophobia
      not in homophobia
      but a crime of hospitality's violation
   as brute history all kindred must admit to
   that *we* were the rapists slavers monsters
Sing of the desolation to know
   the helplessness to be for eternity
   dependent on the hospitality of strangers
   ever a refugee begging asylum
   every land you'll walk in
      lost last citizen of Sodom
Sing of the oath sworn
   that in memory of Mother Sodom
      to redeem her name
   that we should never never never never
   never again deny another stranger
      shelter food
      the couth of ardent kindness
When did it happen this destruction
   Mother Sodom lost in
      vengeance warcrime chance catastrophe
   if not always already
   dead sea valley of salt
      upheaval rout annihilation
   wrought by any Krakatoa or Katrina?
When in all history has Mother Sodom not been burning
   Babylon falling Ilium tumbling
   Jericho into Carthage into
   Dresden into Antioch into
      Sarajevo Guernica Paris
   crumbling rumbling roads of tanks?
When of all crystal moments
   of a grain of salt dissolved

Sodom / New Sodom

    was not contained every tear
        ever wept to look back on loss
    becoming all tears rivered to a Heraklitean torrent
    smashing rapids cataract over a cliff?
When of all dawns
    were we not waking bereft of yesterday's self
    and suddenly other
        under a stranger's roof
    opening curtains to summer rain or winter sun
    crisp frost and grit crunch salty underfoot on the street?
When have we not been
    wandering seeking glancing dancing
    drunk in a London molly house
        San Francisco bathouse
            or Orlando nightclub
    in the days after death
    sworn to live hungry sleep fucked and die trying?
When have we not been
    painting selves as Sebastians
    or mincing as Rosalind as Ganymede as Rosalind
    as actor charging a bard's words
    with a secret shouted open for the gallery:
        and I for no woman!
When have we not been
    weaving our fuckery into eclogues sculptures
        subtexts of agons beefcake photographs
        slashtastic frenemies of fiction myth
    the Bible itself shipping Jonathon and Michelangelo's David?
When have we not been
    making Sodom of the arts in
    winks and wigs of a tapdance
        ballet torchsong musical cabaret Berlin or Broadway
    to welcome wide-eyed twinklings in the stalls
        to sanctuary found?

When Sodom fell for me
   age seventeen in 1988
   ground down by Section 28
      the ravager Saville's
       Iron Lady bosom mate's
   edict forbidding even
      school debate on Section 28
      as breach of Section 28
when I was seventeen and Sodom fell
   a high school hell
      of would-be Columbine
   dissolved to nothing
      at my brother's death
   a hollow child
      black winter howling wild inside
      the wasteland unbound
when I was seventeen and still illegal
   mute in Moloch
   seeking solace in a book
   Delany's Driftglass epigraph lit the light
   with conjured exile's cry for Sodom:
      where now shall we go to make a home?
When I was twenty-one
   and trembling brave to cross a threshold
   I stepped out into a scene
   not home for me but dancing queens
   whose music I abhorred
   black leather rockboy out of place *and yet…*
When I was twenty-one
   and only read of cottages and cruising
   read of constables swooping stings
   and registries of sex offence and HIV and
   O how I hated fucking dance music
      still…

> to be pulled—and pulled *off*—O

When we first wake as Sodomites after Sodom
> all sole survivors
> each of us alone in Zoar
> some have couthie kin ensconcing
> taken aback or wryly smiling
> but resolving deeper love in truth
>> but some do not

When we first take one step
> as child of Sodom then how many
> fledgling souls cast out of Pence's torture camps
> have glimpsed in gay porn the truth of desire
> but never dreamed what's hidden there to find
>> that

when we spread across the Earth
> as Sodom's lost diaspora of millennia
> the work began
> with trade or tristes in the markets
>> couplings in dark parks
>> a cottage claimed
>> a street of pubs and clubs
>> and lo a village! So…

when you look for Mother Sodom
> look around you for our Mother Sodom
> she is here in every city of the world
> beneath each rainbow flag
> as faggot Yeshua under every rock
> and in each broken stick of soul

When did it happen such restoration
> Mother Sodom built anew
> New Sodom risen
> in revelry revelation revolution?
> I say New Sodom is evermade returning
> ever forged in yearning furnace passion burning

When shall we build New Sodom
   if we do not build today
   if we're not building in this second
   every tick and tock of clock
      each breath
   each holy breath the sacred inspiration
   of an advocate for every exile?
When we have built New Sodom
   I for you and you for me
      and thee and they and thou
      and he she *ze*
   for all humanity encompassed in the tiny plural *we*
   then we
      we joyous mob
   we'll be the citizens of love set free
When do we want it?   Now!
When do we need it?   Now!
When will we bring it?   Now!
When will our voices sing it into being?
                        Now!

Now bring me New Sodom
   my Jerusalem my Mecca and my Rome
   my sacred home a pandemonium to the pious
   haven to the hellion rabble
   dogs and sorcerors and fornicators
   fuck the haters:
                      Bring it on!
Now build me New Sodom
   in the earthquake fracturing of Moloch
   in the cracks and nooks between
   in niches and crooks
      love flourishing unseen
   mycelial boom town
      in the interstices blossoming

Sodom / New Sodom

Now bring me New Sodom
    as I bring it in this verse to you
    in a communion of the queer
    a fierce sodality of the abject
    bastioned in punk art and attitude
    rending the fabric of an Empire ending
Now!

•

And with you as citizens of New Sodom we will build
    and with all
        citizens of New Sodom
        we will build
    that for all strangers
        every outcast sibling lost in danger
    every queer in fear beginnng here
        we'll build
And we'll remember that our Sodom came from Canaan
    under the curse of Ham
    who saw his drunken father naked
    idiom for fuckery
    for Ham being fucked emsaculated
    bitch boy damned to slavery
And we'll remember that as ancient rivals
    crowed sweet justice of
    the unmanned Ham's children as chattelry
    that Europe's slavers raping Africa
    painted Ham's Curse on black skin
    made such slaves our kin

And we'll remember that the pious Lot
   fucked his own children too
   another drunk seduced they say
   aye that's abuse's way
      to blame the victim
        blame the wife erased
         and sluts of daughters begging for it
And we'll remember that
   to wed his nameless daughters
   is to cast all wives the husband's child
   infantilising wife-as-peer
   for sham of patriarchy
      fratriarchy's lie
   so I defy denial of our equal sisters
And we'll remember then
   that Sodom's lesson
      is not brotherhood's *no homo* only
   but the bloody birth of fratriarchy
      that excludes by race and gender too
   New Sodom standing as defender then of every *you*
And we'll remember this as fascists march today
We will stand in New Sodom for the queers
   the Texas fags and dykes fearing teacher informants
We will stand in New Sodom for the trans
   of bathroom hysterias and new panic defences
We will stand in New Sodom for the black and brown
   facing death squad cops and registry
   disenfranchisement and deportation
   internment ever rotting into labour camps
We will stand with the socialists
   and anarchists
   as antifascists
   never giving ground
      ¡No pasaran!

Sodom / New Sodom

We will give no ground but take it
   the terrain of history and myth
   pressing on to the last Trump
   to every last Pence spent in shock and awe
   with every last breath holy holy holy
      making holy the profane
      as sacred salt of the earth
We will survey the land of rhetoric and dreams
   stripping tabloid lies to the fresh loam
      digging under dirt to bedrock
      and begin
We will invite to us all strangers still to come
   to feast and rest before the work
   in these first days of a better nation
We will bring it this firelight in dawn's mist
   to gather throng
   in worker's song
      Resist!
And we will build New Sodom for us all.

Made in the USA
Monee, IL
16 January 2021